4.95

D1402710

Children's Portraits in Conté

in Conté

A Lighthearted Approach

GAVIN
Courtesy Mr. and Mrs. Hamilton Rowan, Jr.

Children's Portraits in Conté

A Lighthearted Approach

BY PEGGY HAMMOND

1961

Watson-Guptill Publications, Inc.

NEW YORK

© 1961 BY WATSON-GUPTILL PUBLICATIONS, INC.
New York, New York
Edited by Sterling McIlhany
Designed by Emilio Squeglio
All rights reserved. Printed in U.S.A.
Library of Congress Catalog Card Number 60-13374

To my son,
who never sat still for a minute

FOREWORD

No other subject is as fascinating and challenging to the uncertain hand of the beginning artist as the portrait. There is something about the face in art, especially the face of a child, that works an irresistible charm over us.

For the portrait artist, perhaps no pleasure can match that of capturing on paper the particular expression and personality of childhood. Few other subjects demand so much love or offer such rewards.

Unfortunately, too many drawings of children, however competent they may be technically, are merely shrunken adults, or so overwhelming in their sweetness that they lose all relation to their small models. When we first saw the beautiful drawings of Peggy Hammond, we realized that she was an artist with the rare ability to find and reveal the unique beauty of the face of childhood. Her command of technique—the result of ten years' intensive experience— is a challenge to every student of drawing. Her love and respect for her small subjects, however, make this challenge an inspiration.

With this book Peggy Hammond becomes an author for the first time. Although she professed at first some trepidation at undertaking to instruct others in the art of children's portraits, she soon produced a manuscript which provides not only a wealth of valuable technical information, but succeeds in communicating a delightful sense of fun and excitement in her work. We think you will agree.

CONTENTS

Chapter

INTRODUCTION

One of the more appealing aspects of portrait drawing is that you can have such a wonderful time. I've been drawing portraits for years, but I don't think I have ever once thought of it as work. Almost every portrait has been a happy experience, and every new little face not a challenge but an invitation to enjoy myself. They are not all easy, and an occasional failure can take all the sunshine from your day; but there's no need to give up gloomily after two or three indifferent portraits and take up china painting. Once one good likeness has been accomplished it can be done again. On the next try a parent's eyes will light up and you are on your way.

As happy an experience as a child's portrait can be, it is sometimes hair-raising too. I draw standing up, stepping back, sometimes suddenly, to get the total effect. Many times I have had to use some rather nimble footwork to keep from squashing the customer, who for some reason was standing right behind me, when I thought he was over there somewhere. Everyone pretty much agrees that the fleeting, evanescent quality of childhood is one of its greatest charms. Once I was doing twins, one at a time, and while I was concentrating on some phase of my drawing, the subject would become very fleeting and evanescent indeed and take off silently for the dining room. When I would look around again, her place would have been taken by her sister. They weren't identical and I aged perceptibly that afternoon. It's a lucky thing I like children. Perhaps the prescription for a successful portrait is affection for your work and for your subject.

A picture of a child doesn't have to be a significant social document. A landscape painter, abstract artist, or sculptor must do important work or he will take a panning from the critics and never get to hang in the Museum of Modern Art. You, drawing little faces for which there is a large and ready market, don't have to worry about a thing except getting an attractive likeness. The chances are you won't hang in any museums, but you will hang on a lot of living room walls.

In the final analysis, the so-called serious artist, to a large extent, expresses only himself. He may get thousands of dollars for a landscape (my hat is off to him—I came to the conclusion years ago that only God can make a tree), but he will never see the look in a mother's eyes when her child emerges from a piece of paper at that particular, wonderful instant of babyhood which only the portrait artist can convey.

CHAPTER 1

The Portable Studio

A splendid argument in favor of doing portraits in a one-color medium is that you can carry your studio in your pocket. Oil and pastel artists must have a bewildering array of materials: bottles and jars, easels, north lights, palettes, razor blades, canvases, colored and white paper, smocks (ever see a portrait artist without one?), fixative, brushes, and box after box after box of colors. The line artist, however, needs only a small, inexpensive box of drawing crayons about four inches square, a Pink Pearl, or similar eraser from the dime store, and two pencils, one a drawing pencil, the other any old lead pencil with a good eraser. A toothed paper is superior in effect to a smooth finish, and nearly all art stores have acceptable supplies *(See Manufacturers' List in back)*. Any flat surface is your easel, and, although the light must be good enough to permit you to see your subject, it doesn't have to be from the north. In addition, drawing crayons are clean to work with; you don't need a smock. If you get a little reddish, it will wash off, and thumbprints on the wall can be removed as readily.

Crayons and Pencils

Choosing the color of a one-color medium is up to the individual. I picked the red Conté rather than sepia or black, as the darker tones are a little harsh for portraying children, and the red (sanguine) is not only soothing to the eye but immensely flattering, both to the subject and to the drawing. When I first started, I didn't know that there was any difference in the shades of sanguine, and I couldn't understand why one came out so much darker than another or why I had to use a different approach to shading. I will say I produced some very peculiar effects before I caught on that the number on the box indicated the color of the crayon. I was always dropping the sticks and didn't realize that a stub barely an inch long had at least four portraits left in it; so I bought any box of sanguine that I spied on a shelf. Unknowingly, I might start a portrait with No. 225 (extra soft—a warm orange-red), break the crayon, fumble in my drawing box for another, and finish up the picture with Watteau (No. 228), which is more purple than orange and much harder. No. 225 suits my particular style best, but No. 226 (XVIII Siecle) will do in a pinch, as it is only fractionally darker. Not wanting to be tied to one manufacturer, I tried Eberhard Faber's Nupastel; and their No. 203P is almost identical in color and texture to the Conté. The sticks are a little larger, but I'm blest if I can see any difference in the effect. Somewhere around here I'd like to mention that crayon is a confusing term for sanguine. Crayon, translated from the French, means pencil. Also, sanguine crayons shouldn't be identified with wax crayons. "Crayon" has a sort of a dismal connotation, as it brings to mind references to crayon enlargements of tin-

14

types of the dear departed or the St. Louis World's Fair.

It surprises me that instruction in the use of drawing crayons is so rigid. Smudging is viewed with alarm, and there is much stress on crosshatching, or innumerable fine lines on a paper with a smooth finish. My first crayon was given to me many years ago by an artist who threw in some free advice on how to use it. Bold heavy lines, said he. For contrast one was supposed to use one of those gluey little erasers that children all love to chew, to dig holes in the drawing for chiaroscuro. When the time came for me to make my first portrait, I paid no attention whatever to what I'd been told, and handled the sanguine in the same way I would charcoal, erasing and smudging whenever I felt like it. Who's to say whether that's right or wrong? The cave dwellers drew their fascinating animals with a red chalk medium (forerunner of sanguine), and I'm willing to bet nobody told them they had to crosshatch. Or imagine Toulouse-Lautrec's gentle rejoinder if some teacher came along and told him he couldn't erase when he wanted to.

When I was making my first attempts, I bravely began a portrait using the crayons without making any preliminary sketch. The result almost scared me right out of the art field, as you can't make mistakes and then erase at will. The likeness may eventually be quite striking, but working over and rubbing destroy the freshness of the picture. Most of the pencil companies put out colored drawing pencils which are easy to erase, if you use them lightly, and which are a great help in making the original outline.

Erasers

Using the style I do, I couldn't survive without my Pink Pearl eraser. It costs something silly like fifteen cents and is invaluable, both as an eraser and as a bargaining agent when a small sitter shows signs of becoming intractable. The lead pencil eraser, being small and easily manipulated, is for lighting areas where the larger eraser does not provide enough of a point. There is an eraser on the market in pencil form which you unwind the way you would a charcoal pencil, but if you unwind it too far you end up with a long wobbly tongue of eraser which is hard to control.

15

Paper

Concerning paper, my preference is a bond charcoal paper, possibly the least expensive on the market; my second choice is a French paper called Ingres, manufactured by Ganson et Montgolfier, which is widely distributed in this country. Also nice to work with is a charcoal paper which has less tooth than the other two mentioned. Several companies put out sketch blocks with a texture similar to charcoal paper, but the sheets are smaller, of course, than the ones you can buy singly. In using any of these papers, be sure you hang them right. The watermarked papers should have the emblem to your right, and if you don't have the medallion on the bond paper in the upper left hand corner, your erasures will not only smudge, they will take off the surface. If you are doing more than one portrait in a family, use the same kind of paper for each, as the effect can be quite different with various papers.

Work Surface

As to the easel, by all means use one if you want, but it isn't necessary. For example, I drew five portraits in the cabin of our forty-one foot sail boat, which is hardly as commodious as a studio. An easel there would have been out of the question. A wooden drawing board, because it is lightweight and portable, is perhaps the most convenient drawing surface. It can either be propped up on an easel or placed on any handy piece of furniture.

Some of my searches for flat surfaces, when I am working away from home, have landed me in odd places. Twice I have taped the paper to full-length mirrors and more than twice to a plate-glass window, which can be very exciting. The picture becomes translucent, with the light coming through it, and you really don't know what you have until you take the drawing down. The most ridiculous place I have ever done a portrait was on a sheet of paper tacked onto the swinging door of a kitchen, the whole thing rendered slightly giddy by the fact that the members of the family who were not posing would forget what was going on and come plunging through. All I could think of at the time was the phrase "the likeness hits you right in the face."

16

CHAPTER II

Skull Practice

Develop your own technique. There are several schools of thought on how to go about it. One passionately defends the formal art school, the other as passionately defends the do-it-yourself approach. Good art instruction early in your career certainly can't do any harm in getting you started. You may think my style is perfectly frightful and not want to draw my way at all, but here and there a paragraph may open a door for you that was closed before, and if that is the case I've been of value and you can snort all you like at certain inaccuracies in my execution. You may take lessons in oil when you feel you would rather work in pastel, or vice versa, but what you learn, added to what you can do, is as useful in one field as in another. There is the good soul who spent a year in life class drawing painstaking portraits of plaster casts of Greek statues and ended up painting flower pieces. She did learn, though, by sitting down and drawing what she saw, albeit she never put pencil to head again. On the other hand, there are the artists who paint and paint and paint without any instruction whatever, and some of them eventually put out some interesting work. Some of them don't, too.

I tried to show a picture from its first shaky beginnings to its completion; but having someone breathing down my neck, photographing each phase, was too much for my fragile talent, and I wound up with a horrible mess. It didn't even look like the child. In any case, unless you are a trained teacher, I don't think it's possible to say "do thus and so," as the way I do thus and so varies with each picture. My own instruction was brief and sketchy and I only remember a few of the phrases uttered by George Bridgman when he lectured in life class. When he was doing individual criticism, he uttered no phrases whatever but with a look of complete despair would flip out my drawing with his chamois. He had a way of putting his thumbs in his waistcoat and standing wordlessly behind you (maybe why I can't stand it now). Just when you were about to slit your throat, he would moan "Oh-h-h-h-h-h-h, MISS!" and flop away with the chamois. In my own defense, he always left the head intact.

Preliminary Sketch

In portrait work you really do have to know something about anatomy. You may pick it up in art class or just around the house. It is rare to find someone who has never met an artist or had one in the family somewhere, and, as artists usually have a thing or two to say about art, some of their information is bound to seep into the subconscious. I am assuming here that some of it has seeped in and that you do know the basic measurements of the head. If not, there are several excellent and scholarly books on drawing and anatomy. However, if a book on the subject doesn't happen to be handy, and I've so inspired you that you want to begin the minute your child gets home from school, I'm including some preliminary sketches in various positions. Don't be alarmed if in your first quick sketch the features are placed a little wrong and have to be shifted. I start at the top of the head, and by the time I've placed the eyes, ears, nose, and mouth, I usually discover that the chin is too short or the eyebrows are too close to the eyes. Knowing that the preliminary sketch work is so light that it can be erased completely, I don't worry in the least.

18

In the three-quarter view, profile, and full-face the measurements can be made with straight lines. Generally, the line of the top of the eyes bisects the head. The end of the nose is located halfway between the line of the eyes and the chin. And the mouth usually is placed halfway between the end of the nose and the chin. If the head is tilted, use curved lines to show where the features are placed.

Although you may know your measurements perfectly, it doesn't pay to be too geometric. A child's face is more a matter of curves than angles. Also, you may have absorbed the fact that, roughly, the top of the ear and the top of the upper eyelid are in line, as are the bottom of the ear and the bottom of the nose. Generally speaking, that's dandy, but then along comes your next subject and who is he? Dumbo. You're not going to refuse to draw him because his ears don't fit your preconceived notion of where they should go. Be a little less than faithful in reproducing them. Flattery never hurt a portrait yet.

On the whole, the best way to learn to draw heads is to draw heads. You may never want to do portrait work professionally, but whether you do or you don't, there is no harm in trying to be as expert as your capabilities will allow. The same rule applies to drawing as to playing the piano. Practice. Is there a beguiling red-head down the block? Buy him a banana split to sit for you. He'll be charmed. Draw heads in various positions and apply what you have learned of measurement to the head after you've finished it, and see how close you have come. After enough practice, your picture will be in drawing without any conscious effort on your part. To find out if you're in drawing, hold the picture up to a mirror, or reverse it against a light. It will probably be slightly bulgy, or a little crooked here and there, but if it has charm, relax. After all, if either you or your customer wants a photograph, use a camera, not a pencil.

Speed is a prerequisite in drawing children. The expectancy of childhood won't last through an hour-long pose. A child who has been sitting too long, a bored or a sullen child, isn't going to be wearing an expression worth perpetuating. Train your hand to put down on paper, with as little fuss as possible, what you have trained your eye to see. Make all the mistakes you're going to make in the original outline and get rid of them. With the likeness assured, you can build the portrait as high as you like without resorting to another sitting. If you do need another sitting, it will only be for some forgotten area of shading or something that escaped you in the modeling of the corner of the mouth. And, as it doesn't have anything to do with the basic likeness, an additional sitting will require you to look at the child for only a minute or two.

Working from memory is helpful, particularly to the artist who specializes in children. They have a tendency to vanish when your back is turned, and if you know you're on the right track you don't want to leave your picture to go chasing after them. You don't want them brought forcibly back, screeching, either. Sometimes, after a certain stage in the likeness is past, you can work as well without the child as you can with him. Shut your eyes and visualize his mouth, then draw what you remember. But if you can't, you can't. You may have to use three sittings where someone with a good memory requires only one, but if you don't overwork and if the sittings are short, you can use ten, or twenty, and the picture will still be fresh and charming.

In a field as competitive and challenging as portraiture, you're bound to run into criticism, both constructive and destructive. We love our children. Our customers love theirs. There is a stage in almost every portrait, before its completion, when it's not only necessary, but imperative, to call in the parents for a critical survey. Their objections, if any, may not always be valid, but it isn't up to the artist to say, "This is it," when with a few minor changes it will not only be *it* but a joy forever. Every artist gets stuck sometimes. I owe one of my favorite portraits to a friend who couldn't draw to save her soul, but suggested that the chin was too long. Another time I was troubled and took the picture home to fiddle with it. The man who delivered the bread in that most rural area studied it for awhile and decided I had the cheek sticking out too far. He was right, and here was someone who had neither drawn, nor hoped to draw, a portrait in his life. Then there are the parents who seem to feel that there is a little something wrong with something or other, but can't say what. These I stand behind me, while I wave the pencil at the drawing until they say, "That's it—that's IT!" I haven't changed a line, but they're satisfied. Or if you're doing a picture and have come up with something sort of winsome, you're not going to be as pleased as Punch with the customer who grudgingly admits that the likeness is fine, but doesn't Sally have *four* buttons on her dress, instead of three?

Don't rely too heavily on your own ability as a critic. There's no way of telling what people are going to like. Frequently I find the word "delicate" applied to my work, when I think I'm being angular, modern, and bold.

Several pictures I remember with a shudder, yet the owners appear to be perfectly satisfied with them. One little girl, with a dear little weasel of a face—and incredible eyelashes, turned out such a saccharine mess that I refused to sign her. Nevertheless her portrait is prominently displayed in the parlor, and I've had many complimentary remarks on it from family and friends. But a saccharine mess would never have suited Ellie's mother (*See page 58*); she wanted the long lovely bones and the delicately turned nostril.

CHAPTER III

Sculpture on Paper

Even in optimum circumstances, such as having the right paper, good light, and a cooperative subject, the start of each portrait is like diving off a high board into water you can't see. Though I have done lots of pictures, I'm always convinced that I'm going to be taken with the blind staggers, and nobody is more delighted than I am when the thing starts to take shape.

If a child's portrait is going to be a character study as well as an accurate presentation of the conventional number of features, the artist almost has to bring a newborn viewpoint to each drawing. Just assembling noses and eyes and ears in the right places isn't going to result in a portrait. Therefore, I'm rather pleased when I tremble and die before I make the first fateful stroke, and my excitement over getting something right transmits itself to the subject. She gets in cahoots with me, and if I say, "Whee! I do believe your nose goes right there," she surreptitiously feels it, as if to make sure that it's cooperating, and beams at me.

A drawing medium allows a lot more freedom than a painting

medium. Due to techniques and approaches which have developed over the years, many artists who work in the more fussy media have a tendency to cover every square inch of the canvas with pigment and, unless they are very, very good indeed, may come up with a candy box result. The structure of a child's face interests me more than her golden hair, and I would rather show the bone formation of her forehead than have the thing all cluttered up with hats and coats and backgrounds and kittens and so forth. To me, the drama of a drawing of a child is the drawing itself, not the trimmings. Occasionally you will run into a dubious customer who would rather have Betsy's blue eyes and blonde ringlets faithfully reproduced in color. Knowing that she won't be satisfied with a one-color character study, I send the dubious customer elsewhere. I want people to like my medium as well as what I do with it, and I want my pictures to hang on the wall, not in the attic.

There is danger in being too uncluttered, too. You can draw a splendid likeness with a few deft strokes, but if it vanishes from view at a distance of more than three feet, there is work still to be done. On several occasions I must admit I have been rather sketchier than I planned, but carried away by what I felt was a lively likeness, I had been on the verge of signing, only to have someone come along and say with great enthusiasm, "My! You certainly have made a wonderful start!" That is my cue to amplify a bit. If the start is that good, what I do to bring the picture out isn't going to hurt it any. A picture that is faint, although it may be appealing, can look timid and tentative. Also, without sufficient modeling and shading, either bold or subtle, a portrait drawing can seem very flat.

Shading and Modeling

There are several ways to shade; the method you use is one of personal preference. For a broad, heavy effect you can either bear down hard or use the flat of the crayon, blending the wide lines together and bringing out contrast with the eraser. Innumerable fine lines on a paper with a smooth finish produce a feathery texture. Crosshatching is interesting, but I haven't found that it lends itself too well to the soft contours of a child's face. The technique I use the most is the rubbed finish,

TECHNIQUES OF MODELING AND SHADING

Flat of crayon

Crosshatching

Deep, bold lines with erasure

Smudged with residue on fingers

Drawn

Drawn and rubbed

EXAMPLES OF DRAWING AND RUBBING
TO IMPLY BONE STRUCTURE

High Cheekbone

Fat cheek

where-in you blend the shading with your fingers, again using the eraser for contrast. This produces a very soft and appealing effect, but be careful not to have the rubbed area too large or the lighted area too brilliant, or your drawing will look as though you did it in vaseline. Finally, there is the smudge (I call it that for lack of a better name) applied directly to the paper with the residue of chalk left on your fingers. If controlled, the result is most attractive, but uncontrolled it merely looks as though you didn't know how. Some artists like to use paper stumps in shading, but I agree with the old saying that fingers were made before forks, and they were made before stumps, too.

The slight roughness of a toothed paper makes your shading dramatic without your having to do very much about it. I usually smudge in the shading very lightly until I figure it is in the right places, then deepen it with quick strokes, rubbing later, until I have the effect I want. This is the most entertaining part. But be sure that the likeness is set before you start shading so that what you do will enhance what you have done. In other words, don't do your drawing at the end.

To get the feel of modeling, run your finger from the deep shading at the inside corner of your own eyes around the eye-socket, down

26

Overdrawing and too much rubbing give a vaseline effect

the nose and around the nostril, and from the edge of the eyebrow to the point of the chin. See how you follow a series of curves, not straight lines. Also, feel all those bumpy little bones, which are there even if they don't show. At this stage, modeling is more like sculpture than drawing; while you are working with your fingers, the paper ceases to be a flat surface and becomes three-dimensional. In this semi-soft medium, the residue of crayon on your fingers is of great value. As they are not drawn into the paper yet, smudges applied with your fingers can be easily erased, and you can try a number of effects before hitting the right one without making a muddy mess.

Lighting

In the matter of lighting, it's the general opinion that a work being done in color should be lit from the north. A north light is rather flat, and you don't suddenly get masses of sunlight to change colors and contours. Any light at all, provided it brings out the subject's features to where I, in my near-sighted way, can see them, will do in a one-color medium. In most cases, having the light stronger on one side gives you a stronger portrait, but I have found that a very attractive effect can be achieved if the light comes from below. Entirely by accident on one occasion, the light reflected off a piece of white paper lying on the floor, and I got the above-mentioned effect. On the other hand, if you're going in for a lot of modeling and shading anyway, you can add or subtract it without paying too much attention to what the light is doing. It may be full on the face of the subject, but once you know how, modeling can be added where needed to keep the picture from being too flat. I generally leave fairly large areas of the paper uncolored or merely rubbed very lightly to give an impression of skin tones, so any shading I do needn't be particularly bold.

In a one-color medium, strong electric light (not special daylight bulbs or anything—just an unshaded lamp) is as good as sunlight. The shadows cast are perhaps a little deeper, but you can lessen those if you want to. It all really boils down to whether you can see your subject, and it doesn't matter much how you go about it. I'm blind as a bat, so I have trouble seeing both subject and paper, and therefore don't usually work on a gray day. On a wet day I won't even work with electric light. Dampness has a distressing effect on all the charcoal papers; the crayons come out very dark, and erasure is almost impossible.

Eyes

Eyes are the most important. If you haven't got the eyes you haven't got anything. Get the outline the way you want it, darken the line of the upper lid, add the eyelashes with light strokes, and then place the iris—lightly, though. Mistakes here could be fatal. Even with very pale eyes, making the top of the iris slightly darker than the bottom gives an impression of depth, and in any eye, light or dark, don't overdo the

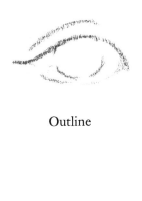

Outline

Accents

Placement

Expression

pupil. One brilliant highlight is inevitable, but to get a laughing or a liquid effect try lighting the eye from several directions. The purists will scream, but it makes a very attractive looking eye.

Children's eyelashes are highly improbable, and although it's clumsy to make them look mascaraed don't be over-cautious. Perhaps I go a little strong on eyelashes, but I can't bear to leave them out.

Ears

On the subject of ears, set them in properly in the beginning and then forget them until the relatively more difficult lines of character and expression have been attended to. Ears don't wiggle or change their appearance and can safely be left to the last. But don't assume that when you've drawn one ear, you've drawn them all. Some flap, some lie close to the head; some have long, and some have no, lobes. They may be pointed, or the tops may turn over. The safest rule to follow is not to embroider them. It isn't necessary, as long as the shape and the setting are right, to depict every channel and ridge.

Hair

Hair in a one-color medium can be the most difficult part of all. Here your eraser really counts. There are few things to equal the freshly washed look of childhood's hair, and with shading and erasure you can approximate the sheen. For very fair hair, use your fingers, with their faint residue of crayon, to indicate the shaded areas. Putting a series of soft smudged lines from crown to forehead, in the case of bangs for instance, and then drawing the eraser right across them will give the impression of blondeness. Red hair I rub and smudge with a linen handkerchief, which seems to pick up the orange tones in the crayon more than fingers; and I light it as much as possible. With brown hair I don't use the handkerchief but do use a good deal of light; and with black hair, the bolder the lights and darks the better. A crew cut is something else. The first one I tried was a success due to the suggestion of the subject's brother. He saw me looking nervously at the velvety head and asked me how I proposed to do it. I answered truthfully that I didn't have the faintest idea. "Think of grass," he said, "and then mow it."

Somewhere in the dim and misty past someone told me that in drawing hair you should always show stray strands flying around, whether they're there or not. No matter how much a child's hair has been recently brushed and plastered down, there are always elflocks. I'm particularly enamored of the wisps on the forehead, which for some reason appear mostly to be the province of blondes. Cowlicks are something of a trial, too. The ones on the back of the head are easy, but preserve me from the ones on the hairline. The light catches them in such a way that if you try to erase and smudge them into existence, it looks as if the poor little boy had a bald spot.

HAIR TREATMENT

Fly-away blonde hair using the same approach

Smudging and light erasure give effect of blonde bangs

Mouth

By smudging and using the pointed eraser, indicate dimples around an otherwise serious mouth. A set, closed mouth doesn't give a particularly good impression of childhood, so, though I do usually have the child's mouth closed, I leave out as much as I put in. The outline isn't all that important—it's the expression that counts. A young friend of mine, completely undone by her first baby, finally went to the doctor to find out why her little darling's mouth was always hanging ajar. He kindly assured her that it was merely the law of gravity. After two the tendency to gape departs, which is one of the reasons I would just as soon not attempt to draw anyone younger than that. Very small babies have all the necessary features, but they slip and slide, making it very hard to capture their particular expression. A shaded line below the lip will give the optical illusion of carrying the lip all the way to the corner of the mouth without actually putting in the outline.

A good example of my mouth technique is the terrified Teresa, in Head Hunting. She was scared green during the entire pose and wouldn't look directly at me for a second. I don't think I've told so many jokes all in a row in years, and finally, although her eyes still mirrored impending doom, I was able to coax the beginnings of a small, reluctant smile.

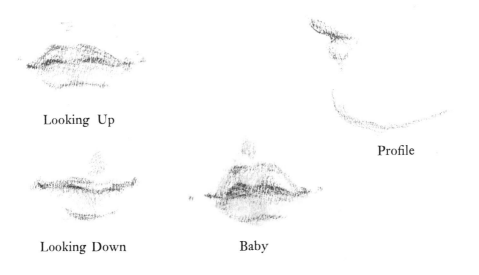

Looking Up

Profile

Looking Down   Baby

Nose

Children aren't noted for the bridges of their noses—concentrate on the curve of the nostril, or the snub end of a nose, indicating the bridge with the faintest of shadows.

To imply a snub, I usually just run my finger across the bridge, lighting with the eraser if necessary, as in the case of both Libby and Steve. Some nostrils are more apparent than others. The Haitian baby is looking up a little, so discounting the African influence on his features (he *is* a boy, in spite of his hat), the nostril has to be fully described. In the little blonde looking down, the nostril is mentioned only in passing, so to speak, with two lines.

There is usually a sort of shiny place on the end of a little nose, which is best executed with the small eraser. Other good spots for light are on the lower lip and the line of the jaw, to add contrast to the shading of the cheek. But with light as well as with shade you have to be careful. A light in the wrong place can change the whole aspect of your drawing. It can make a rounded cheek look pouchy or focus the eyes in such a way that one looks one way and one another, or make an earlobe stick out like a searchlight. If I stand well back and the eyes laugh right at me and the chin doesn't disappear into the neck, yet there isn't a harsh or a heavy line, I can call it a day.

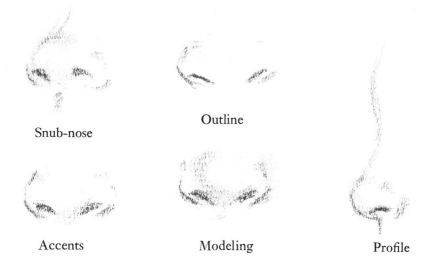

Snub-nose

Outline

Accents

Modeling

Profile

Chin

Chins are like ears; don't feel that if you've drawn one you've drawn them all. There are dimpled chins, receding chins, double chins, rounded or pointed chins. A cleft one is fascinating, all the more so in the case of the true cleft, which even cleaves slightly the lower lip, the end of the nose, and, in extreme cases, the forehead. It's an interesting thing for an artist, as it proves the rule about basic measurements you apply to the head, viz: bisection. We do bisect the head, either mentally or on the paper, while making the original sketch, but it has been demonstrated over and over that one side of an individual face is dramatically different from the other. If you drew one side, and then creased the paper down the middle and made an exact copy of the side you had drawn, you'd have difficulty recognizing your subject. The beginner will look at a pair of eyes and think they are the same size and shape, when they aren't at all. I've known people with one brown eye and one blue eye. Fascinating. But that's an obvious difference which anyone can see. The subtlety of a left eye that slants while the right eye is as round and guileless as a marble is up to the artist to capture without caricature. One of the most attractive children I have ever known was born out of drawing. Her eyes were on different levels, her nose slanted to the left, her mouth to the right, and the result, instead of being frightening, was utterly bewitching.

CHAPTER IV

Quicksilver vs. Rigor Mortis

Some children are saintly about sitting still for at least as long as it takes to block in the sketch; some are too young, and some simply don't want any part of it. The latter you can usually bring around in time. Children would rather be friendly than not. However, there are some who are beastly from start to finish. In such a case, think of what kindergarten teachers go through and be brave. Somewhere amid all those howls and scowls lurks the look the parents want you to see.

An artist friend of mine has a system of painting the very young while they're immobilized at lunch, but I find that the characteristic bulge of childhood's cheek loses much of its charm when enhanced by the characteristic bulge of mashed potato. On the whole it's easier for me to paddle around after the very little ones, trusting to memory and speed to get the likeness.

Feeling particularly agile one day, I tackled the portrait of Geoffrey, aged two. I had several aged-two size chairs and a selection of toys waiting, also television and a tempting (I thought) corner of the sofa piled high with pillows. They held his interest only momentarily. No matter how rapidly I worked, when I looked up he'd be halfway up the stairs, or under the sofa, or composing on the piano in the subdominant. Occasionally, if I'd wanted to, I could have made a magnificent portrait of the seat of his overalls—or the soles of his shoes. Inspiration finally came in the form of a very fancy hat from Jamaica. It fascinated him. It also obliterated him, as he chose to wear it on his face, but by peering under it I got what I had missed while trying to draw entirely from memory and at a dead run. The hat never had to come off completely, as I'd already had a good look at his hairline when he was behind the Hi-Fi.

The accompanying photographs present Geoffrey, the Hat, and the Hairline, the like of which, I'm sure, have never been seen before on land or sea. I used my friend's system at the very end, but with cookies, not lunch. Luckily I had finished the mouth; a chocolate moustache has its place, but that place is not in one of my pictures. At that, Geoffrey was easier than the next two year old who came my way. He sat like a little statue. At all times, and with both hands, he clutched his nose.

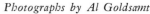

Photographs by Al Goldsamt

Geoffrey's Idea of a Pose

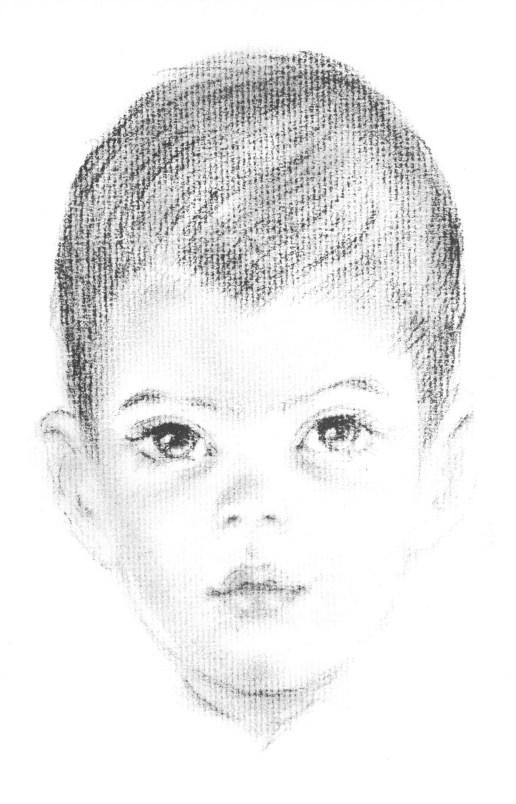

GEOFFREY

Courtesy Mr. and Mrs. Paul Grevé

Older children are harder in a sense than little ones. If two will hardly pose at all, twelve will pose too much. No matter how attractive, appealing, handsome and lively twelve is, when he sits down to be drawn he dies right in front of your eyes. A taxidermist could hardly make him look more stuffed. He will do exactly as he's told, moving his head a painful fraction of an inch, his teeth and fists clenched, his eyes glazed. I'm not making a death mask, therefore it's up to me to resuscitate the body. So I talk. I babble. I blither. If he answers, the end is in sight. If he laughs, the battle is won. Twelve's eyes will light up just as much as two's, and you can draw an awfully attractive mouth when it still has the memory of a laugh in the corners.

On that subject, drawing a laughing child, unless you are remarkably skillful, can be difficult, and the result downright unpleasant. It's better to imply the beginning or the end of a smile than to draw a face full of teeth. Teeth are sometimes unavoidable; you get lots of little squirrels and beavers in the course of your career, but I minimize them as much as possible.

Another problem which comes up occasionally is that of a cast in the eye. A child is her own lovable self, but there are no two ways about it—she's cross-eyed. When that happens, a three-quarter view is preferable to full-face. It lessens the effect of the cast without leaving it out entirely.

Anybody over two will hold still long enough to be posed to the greatest advantage, and once the outline is drawn, three, four, or six can whiz around the place as much as two and, not having been made unhappy by sitting still too long, will give you a pleasant expression when called back for a minute. The in-between ages, say from four to ten, compared to the others, are a cinch. Old enough to respond, they're young enough to stay alive. A little girl of seven, not sure what's about to happen to her or whether it will take too many of her precious hours of freedom, will suddenly discover that it doesn't hurt a bit and that it's even fun. You can get a really entrancing portrait of someone who's enjoying herself. Or maybe Jimmy is in a snit. After getting the outline, ignoring the frown and the cold, disapproving eyes, I tell him to go away and come back with a different face. Almost invariably he thinks that's funny. Of course, some of the faces he brings back are not exactly

STEVE
Courtesy Mrs. Harriett Barber

what his parents had in mind, but it cheers him up.

In posing it's important for a child of any age to be as comfortable as possible. All I need is my flat surface and enough room to back away from the picture, but he can loll at his ease in a luxurious arm chair, or a sofa, or anywhere the light hits him. My own house is an elderly saltbox, with all the quaintness and charm of low ceilings and tiny window panes, but dark as your pocket. There is one room with adequate light, but due to a condition involving the placement of the furniture, the only flat surface is so situated that I have to draw draped over the television. So I prefer to go to the subject's own house. There's another good reason for that. A child is much more apt to be happy and relaxed in familiar surroundings.

A flow of conversation doesn't do any harm, and I talk *to* the children, not *at* them. If the two of us are having a fascinating discourse on the subject of birthdays, I can interrupt long enough to say, "Whoa. You're collapsing. Lift your chin a little," without sounding bossy. I try to keep the whole thing as informal as possible, letting them take a look whenever curiosity overcomes them. Once I was doing a little girl with a charmingly bushy head of dark hair, and it did seem to me that I was getting a good, affectionate likeness. Imagine my horror when I invited Miss Bushy to take a look, and she instantly burst into roars of dismay. Between the sobs, I was finally able to distinguish the words "But my hair isn't red!" Settling that took diplomacy and an eraser. Later, when exhibiting her portrait to friends who had the same criticism, she was heard to say grandly, "It's the meemium that's red, not my hair."

People are always talking about artistic temperament, but I'm personally convinced that we have the patience of Job. But two things really do make me explode. One is the parent or guardian who says "Look at the lady, darling," and darling, who is in a particularly appealing position, moves and freezes into another which is not appealing at all. The other is if anyone gets behind me when I'm drawing and just stands there without saying anything. One father even went so far as to stand behind me and consume a large dish of stewed pears with appropriate sound effects, but with no comments on the progress of the portrait. On the other hand, if he'd made one delighted remark the

LIBBY

Courtesy Mr. and Mrs. Hamilton Rowan, Jr.

musical pears wouldn't have bothered me a whit. Everyone needs encouragement.

To prove my point about patience, I have drawn pictures while lunch parties were in progress, at large family gatherings with the Sunday papers all over the floor, and once, while working on the daughter of the house, I assisted at the accouchement of a remarkably prolific cocker spaniel. That was a day. The maternity ward was in the basement, the studio on the second floor, and the parents, not realizing that the Blessed Event was imminent, had gone Christmas shopping. But they named one of the puppies after me.

A point I haven't brought up at all is figure work. Your child sprawls on the hearthrug, doing his homework, or stands for a moment looking earnestly at a bug in the garden. The only unconscious grace to equal it is that of a major league outfielder. Everything a child does unconsciously is graceful, and everything in his face, no matter how homely, is beautiful. If you're going to be a portrait artist and draw children, see in each child what makes Momma love him. It's there.

CHAPTER V

Tragicomedies

Misfortunes and accidents will happen, and all but a few are un-avoidable. Avoidable, but most disheartening, is bad framing. A drawing on paper must be backed before it's framed; if not, usually in a week or two, the paper buckles behind the glass and wide shallow wrinkles go across the surface. I don't do my own framing, being singularly unhandy, and if my gift wrappings are any criterion, I'd make a dismal mess of cutting a mat. But I have my pet framers, and each one mounts the drawing on stiff cardboard. First they lay the picture flat and moisten the back to soften the fibres. They leave it untouched for about half an hour and then dampen it again. Then, using a loose glue, they cover the entire back of the picture, press it onto the stiff board, weight it to keep it from buckling, and leave it to dry. An unfixed drawing holds no terrors for them, as they know that if the picture doesn't move around while it's lying on its face it won't smudge. Actually, most of them prefer a picture to be unfixed. If it's already been sprayed with fixative they can't do a professional job of cleaning it, and fingerprints, smears, and eraser crumbs are irrevocable.

I love to go into frame shops. People are becoming less and less conservative, and the narrow black frames and plain white mats we can all remember on Grannie's etchings have given way to shadow boxes, carving, driftwood, or almost anything you can think of that will hang. In the matter of mats, it used to be very elegant, but rather daring, to have a French line (a slender colored line about one-fourth inch from the opening) on a mat; but nowadays, considering the burlaps and the linens and the grasscloths, French line seems rather quaint and old-fashioned. Personally, I think this is all a step in the right direction. For their impact, my pictures have the contrast between the head and a large amount of white background. In a plain frame, a grasscloth or linen mat enhances the contrast without overwhelming the drawing. You'd better go easy on very dramatic mat materials, though, if the frame itself is ornate or very wide.

Some of my misadventures in the art world are rather farfetched. One doesn't usually expect floods, for instance, but I lost a portrait to Long Island Sound when an unprecedented high tide floated into the living room. When it receded, the water mark was so high there were mussels in the piano and my picture was wearing a beard of salt hay.

Another flood which cost me dear was man-made. Cindy began playing that lovely game where you shake a full coke bottle. That one flooded me, too. Probably the noisiest accident I ever had was when my dog, his instincts too much for his manners, chased my new cat right through a drawing, which for some reason I had propped up in a wing chair. I had bought the cat for a dollar from the Animal Shelter because of mice, but he left right after that and adopted a neighbor. I still have mice and I had to do the picture over.

However, these are things that would only happen once in a blue moon. Everyday sorts of accidents, like wrinkles and grease spots, are exasperating because they can happen so easily. Whatever you're using for an easel, be sure the picture won't fall off. If I can't use thumbtacks, I use scotch tape, and if there isn't any of that, bandaids will do, if you use enough of them. An insecurely hung paper, in falling, almost always picks up a deep wrinkle in the wrong place which even the most expert framer views with alarm. Grease spots are horrible and sometimes appear

CINDY
Courtesy Mrs. Harriett Barber

for no reason at all. The largest source of supply is usually a very young subject who fingers the drawing when your back is turned. If he's had any recent contact with mayonnaise or peanut butter you have to start over again. I generally avoid having lunch with the customer, as I shouldn't be exposed to mayonnaise either.

Incidentally, the retailer sells paper in flat sheets, and, ideally, it should be kept flat when you take it home. However, for reasons of storage economy, it may have to be rolled. This is perfectly safe, both before and after it has been drawn on; but when storing it, be sure it's in a place where the roll will stay round. Once it's been sat on or squashed in any way, it is completely useless. Not that it's terribly expensive, but it's maddening to have to go out and buy some more.

CHAPTER VI

Head Hunting

Working on commission only has a tendency to make one forget all about art, except as a means of making a living. When I feel that I'm becoming too commercial or too bogged down in daily living to draw, I go head hunting. I carry some crayons with me wherever I go; there are always several stubs in my purse. However, carrying a large roll of paper with me at all times has its drawbacks, so I compromise by keeping a sketching block in the car. Inevitably, of course, I find a perfect head when I have nothing to draw on but an old envelope.

In head hunting I use several methods. For instance, I see a little girl with fascinating bone structure dubiously inspecting some unripe bananas in a supermarket. I get out the old envelope, draw a quick study, and amplify and embellish it later from memory. On the other hand, I may approach the head directly and ask its mother if her little boy or girl will sit for me at a certain time. Sometimes they think I'm mad, but usually they comply.

In head hunting you can do one thing which you shouldn't even consider when drawing a commissioned portrait. For practice on different types, you can copy photographs. The chances are you're not going to run into an Eskimo in Grand Central Station, but there may well be an enchanting picture of one in the National Geographic. Using photographs in commissioned work implies a lack of skill, and the result, by the very nature of things, is wooden and static. For the record, all of the pictures on these pages are of actual children I have met in my wanderings, but I have a sketchbook full of heads I have done from photographs.

The practice of using photographs when doing animals is something else. Few dogs or cats, no matter how well-trained, are in the least interested in holding still long enough for any kind of drawing to be made, and, though undoubtedly restful in effect, a sleeping animal hasn't much life to it. I tried a dog once without benefit of camera, and I don't think I'll ever forget it. Beyond a doubt, that was the hardest job I have ever had. There were two little girls on the paper, with a collie between. In my recollection, the picture must have taken at least a week and about nine sheets of paper. First I would get one little girl absolutely perfectly, and then something hideous would happen and the other would be all wrong and erased so much that she was subtly a different color. Finally I got them both the way I wanted them and started in on the dog. With some trepidation I pencilled him in as lightly as I could, at least to get him the right size and in the right place, and then started to fill him in. After hours of honest toil, there rigidly between the two

MATILDA

girls sat Man O' War, with a ruff. Eventually it turned out all right, but my next canine customer, a German shepherd, I got verbatim from a can of dog food, putting his own particular expression on later. However, if you have a great desire and/or aptitude for drawing dogs, there are extremely informative and well-illustrated books on the subject.

Head Hunting sets an artist free from the purely commercial. It's also a form of expression that satisfies the soul because it's being done for the sheer love of doing it. It is more blessed to give than to receive, and the creative artist has unlimited opportunities to be blest. Going on the assumption that a picture is worth a thousand words, artists often donate to charity drives. In my case, being a child specialist, I like to do this for any and all drives by agencies devoted to helping handicapped or homeless children. That's one way of giving. Another is to draw her child for someone you like. Money is all very fine, but a good picture that's made someone happy means as much to me when I give it away as when I get paid for it. Setting a price on a picture exasperates me, anyway. How can you decide what it's worth? It may *cost* nothing and be worth a million, or vice versa.

In some cases, as seen in the pictures that follow, you make a finished portrait, in others a quick sketch, a line drawing, or you may even try a new technique.

HAITIAN BABY

TERESA

BARBARA

Everywhere you go there are pretty children, so-called "cute" children, appealing children, attractive children. Anything under twenty with golden curls is called beautiful when in fact true beauty is so rare that when you run across it it takes your breath away. Barbara is a child like this. Even a quick pencil sketch can capture the Mediterranean beauty of line and structure with still, dark eyes and classic nose.

MANUEL

Manuel is the eight year old son of the gardner who came to see if anything
could be done to my half-acre of crabgrass and clam shells. I have the reverse
of a green thumb. Flowers come up, take one shocked look at me, and go right
back down again. Manuel was solemn for a while but broke down when our
dog carefully dug a hole behind my three petunias and then lay down, partly
in the hole, but mostly on the petunias. The merry mood stayed with him
long enough for this sketch.

NANCY

Nancy at eight months had so many heavenly expressions that I spent a happy hour drawing them all. With a baby of this age, you get all the slipping and sliding mentioned earlier. So the problem is to capture one good expression as quickly as possible and stay with it, with the hope that, sooner or later, she'll get back to it.

DRUCIE

Drucie, aged nine, invaded our boat in Miami one time to borrow the dinghy. She insisted on calling my dog Old Yaller, when in very fact he was titled The Emperor Concerto; but it was her only flaw. She was lively, lovely, and fun to be with. I gave her unlimited use of the dinghy in return for posing.

   She differs in technique in several ways. For one thing, this finished drawing was made on tinted paper, which necessitated the use of white pastel for highlights in the eyes. Her hair was a challenge, being straight, rather long, and wet (she lived on a boat). To give her rather lank hair a feeling of body, I created highlights with the eraser and took some liberties with its length.

ELLIE
Courtesy Mrs. Jane Harding Straus

CONCLUSION

An artist's career is a satisfying one. You're doing what you like to do, getting paid rather handsomely for it, and you can't help but meet attractive, interesting people. If you travel about as I do, you also pick up all kinds of wonderful ideas in decorating, curtain materials, and sauces. Coincidences abound. You're always falling over someone you went to school with, or who went to school with your husband. One coincidence, that gave me something of a fright, occurred while I was doing the older two children in a family of three. There was a sitter for the baby, and perched silently on a sofa was what I took to be the sitter's grandfather. To my embarrassment, he turned out to be not only the customer's uncle, but my own first cousin, once removed.

The parents are fun to meet and get to know, and so are the children. In some places I hope the picture will go slowly, so that I can prolong the odd intimacy which arises. Sometimes, though, you'll get all tangled up with a horror who treats you abominably and whom you despise, though you will sicken yourself calling her "dear" and smiling until your face aches, when what you really want to do is drop-kick her into the next county. If the picture doesn't go, as it probably won't with that kind of an atmosphere, GO AWAY. Make another appointment, and the chances are that the horror will greet you with a smile of pure delight, and you will finish loving her as much, if not more than, all the rest. I remember so many little faces with affection, and can't entirely disassociate myself and my portrait from the child. Thus I look upon myself as the proud parent of some two hundred and fifty children, give or take a dozen or so.

Atmosphere is as important as anything else. A formal house and a starched child I try to deformalize as quickly as possible. Part of my lack of interest in clothes and lace collars is due to my theory that an uncomfortable subject is going to result in a fussy portrait. I therefore recommend T-shirts, and if there is a particular collar or dress to be included, I hang it up on a hanger and draw it in later. The happiest

59

surroundings are the informal ones. I remember with particular warmth two houses, one near Boston and the other high in the hills of New Hampshire. Everybody liked everybody so much and the houses were so full of affection that, although in both cases the light really wasn't very good, my paper seemed to be lit from within.

Of course, some of the people you meet make your hair stand on end. Early in my career one lady took me on as a sort of a protégée. I had just started one of the commissions she had arranged for me, when she came along, shook her head, and said, "No. Won't do. Not big enough." Too new at the game to snarl something about not charging by the yard, I meekly started over. Another time I had a commission that lasted for days, and as I was many miles from home, my dog and I spent the weekend. He was as busy as I was, digging a hole in the lawn and barking furiously at the gardener and the chauffeur whenever he saw them. However, he thoroughly ingratiated himself with my hostess, and when the time came for us to go, she looked him firmly in the eye and said, "YOU may come again."

When you've been working along for a number of years as an amateur, the switchover to professional can sometimes be frightening. Once you're discovered, people have a tendency to speak of you in a hushed voice as if you were dead. "She's different—she paints." But at that, being embalmed is better than being hanged in effigy. Sometimes you drop the ball without knowing it, and the word of your failure travels faster than the shot that was heard round the world. The bad picture you did (and who hasn't done a few of those?) is the one that wakes you screaming in the night. The hanging-in-effigy isn't entirely the province of the professional. Once, while still an amateur, I drew a portrait which I thought was rather lovely, although I knew perfectly well that the eyes were too far apart. However, the parents were charmed, and on the strength of it, asked us to dinner. We should have stayed home. By the time the assembled relatives got through, this was the worst portrait of any child, anywhere, ever, and I know they wouldn't have considered being that beastly about the dress I had on. For all I know, the portrait is still hanging over the mantelpiece and for all I know one of my favorite earrings is still lost under a sofa cushion. I've never had enough nerve to go back and find out.

I'm not a versatile artist. The years have proved to me that I'm a specialist in children, and no matter how hard I try, my portraits of grownups make them all look like elderly babies. And I do try. One friend of mine, delighted with the pictures I had done of her two children, wheedled and coaxed me into trying one of her. The first attempt had a strong flavor of George Washington, aged about eight. Being a descendant of George, she thought that rather amusing, but her friends' reactions were negative. Several years later I tried her again, feeling that maybe I had matured. This time I managed to leave out George, but the general effect was still that of a toddler, and tipsy as well. That may have been because the improvised studio was a cocktail lounge on top of a New York hotel. Because it was a warm day, the doors to the terrace were open. I have often had to dodge children, pets, and furniture. This is the only time I had to be careful about stepping on pigeons.

In conclusion, I go right back to what I said in the beginning. Have fun with art. You and what you do will be better if you have a light heart.

There isn't any foolproof way to be an artist. You need talent, you need work, and you need time. Talent you have, or you wouldn't consider trying to be an artist in the first place. Work you do, because if you have talent you are inwardly compelled to draw and generally start at a very early age. I have no doubt that Renoir was spanked for scribbling on the walls. Time, most of all, is kind to the artist. Without doing anything about it at all, you improve with the passage of years. The four year old who scribbles on the walls is the mature artist of thirty, and the mature artist of thirty may well be a genius at sixty. There just isn't any place to go but up.

ART MATERIALS MANUFACTURERS' LIST

PAPERS, PENCILS AND PASTELS

American Crayon Co.

Conté Pencil Co.

Joseph Dixon Crucible Co.

Eagle Pencil Co.

Eberhard Faber Pencil Co.

A. W. Faber-Castell Pencil Co., Inc.

Frances M. Moore Co.

General Pencil Co.

M. Grumbacher, Inc.

Koh-i-noor Pencil Co., Inc.

Morilla Co.

Reliance Pen and Pencil Corp.

J. S. Staedtler and Co.

Strathmore Paper Co.

Swan Pencil Company, Inc.

Talens and Son, Inc.

Venus Pen and Pencil Corp.

Weber Costello Co.